Heart of Gold

By Kerri Strug
with Greg Brown

Illustrations by
Doug Keith

Taylor Publishing
Dallas, Texas

Greg Brown has been involved in sports for 30 years as an athlete and award-winning sportswriter. Brown started his Positively For Kids series after being unable to find sports books for his own children that taught life lessons. He is the co-author of *Sheryl Swoopes: Bounce Back; Mo Vaughn: Follow Your Dreams; Steve Young: Forever Young, Bonnie Blair: A Winning Edge; Cal Ripken: Count Me In; Troy Aikman: Things Change; Kirby Puckett: Be the Best You Can Be* and *Edgar Martinez: Patience Pays.* Brown regularly speaks at schools and can be reached at: pfkgb@aol.com. He lives in Bothell, Washington, with his wife, Stacy, and two children.

Doug Keith provided the illustrations for the best-selling children's book *Things Change* with Troy Aikman, *Count Me In* with Cal Ripken Jr., and *Forever Young* with Steve Young. His illustrations have appeared in national magazines such as *Sports Illustrated for Kids*, greeting cards, and books. Keith can be reached at his Internet address: atozdk@aol.com.

Kerri Strug would like to give a special thank-you to her family for the constant love and support they have always provided. Additionally, she would like to thank her attorney Leigh Steinberg, for his guidance and invaluable counsel and Stefani Wanicur for her special attention. Without their contributions, this book would not have been possible.

Kerri has made a personal contribution to Special Olympics International, in support of its gymnastics programs for athletes with mental retardation, from the royalties received from the publication of this book.

To visit Kerri on America Online, use the Keyword "Athlete Direct" for access to Kerri's AOL area. To visit Kerri on the Internet, go to www.strug.com.

Published by Taylor Publishing Company
1550 West Mockingbird Lane
Dallas, Texas 75235

Designed by David Timmons

Library of Congress Cataloging-in-Publication Data

Strug, Kerri, 1977–
    Heart of gold / by Kerri Strug with Greg Brown; [illustrated by Doug Keith].
        p.   cm.
    Summary: The young woman who helped the U.S. women's gymnastics team win a gold medal at the 1996 Olympics in Atlanta describes her lifelong interest in the sport and the lessons it has taught her.

    ISBN 0-87833-976-0
    1. Strug, Kerri, 1977–   —Juvenile literature. 2. Women gymnasts—United States—Biography—Juvenile literature. 3. Olympic Games (26th : 1996 : Atlanta, Ga.)—Juvenile literature.
[1. Strug. Kerri, 1977– . 2. Gymnasts. 2. Women—Biography. 4. Youth's writings.] I. Brown, Greg. II. Keith, Doug, ill. III. Title.
GV460.2.S77A3 1996
796.44'092—dc20
[B]
                        96-45070
                        CIP
Printed in the United States of America

10   9   8   7   6   5   4   3   2   1

My name is Kerri Strug, and I've dedicated 14 years of my young life to gymnastics.

The demanding sport has given me lots of wonderful memories along with a few disappointments.

I've written this book to share my story with you so you can learn from what I've experienced and, hopefully, be inspired by my victories.

Dominique Moceanu

Dominique Dawes

Amy Chow

Amanda Borden

Jaycie Phelps

Kerri Strug

Shannon Miller

Walter Iooss, Jr./Sports Illustrated

Few people knew my name before the 1996 Summer Olympics in Atlanta, even though I competed at the elite level for five years and helped the USA earn a bronze medal at the 1992 Barcelona Olympics.

I entered the Atlanta Centennial Games not knowing what to expect. Shannon Miller and Dominique Dawes were the well-known veterans and Dominique Moceanu was the rising young star. Some dubbed me the "stepsister to the stars" because it seemed my career had been overshadowed by others.

Of the seven members on our 1996 American team, only Amy Chow and I were true amateurs. You can only retain amateur status by never accepting money for competitions, showcases, or commercial endorsements. I never took the money because only amateurs are allowed to compete in college and I planned to compete at UCLA as a college gymnast.

Despite my successes leading up to the games, I had a reputation for not performing at my best under pressure.

Several people involved with gymnastics would criticize me because my nervousness sometimes hindered my performance.

Others questioned my mental toughness and ability to handle pain. My coach, Bela Karolyi, used to tease me by calling me "the baby."

One vault in Atlanta changed everything.

Millions watched on television the evening of July 23, 1996, when we entered our final team event. Team USA owned a comfortable lead. Only the vault, a springboard leap over a padded metal horse, stood between us and history. The American women had never won Olympic gold in team gymnastics.

After Moceanu unexpectedly fell twice on her vault, it was my turn. I was the last to jump and everyone believed victory rested on my shoulders.

But I fell on my first vault and heard a pop in my left ankle. A jolt of pain ran up my leg.

I had only seconds to decide what to do. Should I jump again to try and help the team win gold or stop and save myself for the individual competition days later?

I did what my heart told me was right. To fully understand what I felt, let me tell you about events that led to that memorable moment.

When I was born in Tucson, Arizona, in 1977, gymnastics had been part of our family for years. My older brother, Kevin, and older sister, Lisa, were gymnasts long before me.

I always looked up to my brother and sister, especially Lisa. We had a special bond. I liked everything she liked—clothes, food, music, you name it.

I remember going to Kevin and Lisa's gymnastics meets as a toddler and sitting motionless in the stands for hours. I'd intently watch each routine and, as I grew older, I'd keep score on my own.

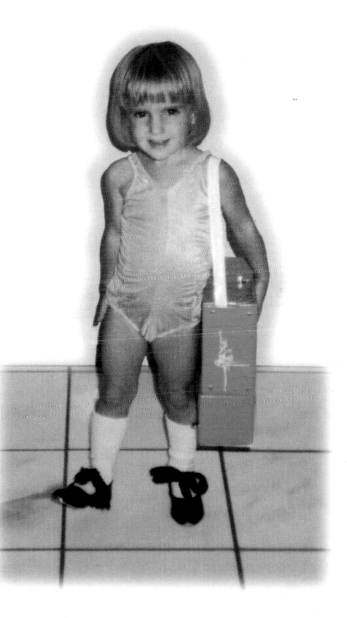

Mom loved ballet and secretly hoped Lisa and I would love it, too. I took dance lessons when I was four years old. But by then, gymnastics was already my favorite.

My parents, Burt and Melanie, had the wisdom to let us try different things and then found the courage to allow us to follow our own interests.

Some kids are pushed into gymnastics by their parents. My parents never pushed me into the sport. I always pulled them, each step of the way.

Ask my parents what I was like as a child, and they'll tell you I was a little daredevil.

I have an assortment of scars from falls I took well before gymnastics.

I needed stitches in my forehead after speeding on a tricycle through our house and ramming into a dresser. I gashed my head roller skating, cut my chin jumping off a swing in kindergarten, and sliced my knee playing on our backyard swing set. Going down slides sitting down wasn't for me; I'd balance on my feet.

Staying on my feet around the house was another matter.

We had one carpeted room in our house that didn't have any furniture. I adopted it as my own private gym. I'd spend hours in that room tumbling and walking on my hands, copying the moves I'd seen my sister do.

"Kerri, please walk with your feet. You're always traveling upside down," Dad would say.

The day my parents filled the room with furniture and took away my "gym" I was so upset I cried.

Kerri with Tracee Talavera in Oregon, where Lisa was training at the same gym.

Lisa   Kerri

I started taking gymnastics classes at age three. I'd tag along with Lisa, who worked out in Tucson with a team called Desert West.

It all felt so natural. Even after hours in the gym, I'd come home and tumble on the carpet or use the lines from our hallway tiles as a pretend balance beam.

Being around my sister gave me a great head start. I still remember the day she taught me how to do a back walkover.

Soon, Lisa and I switched to private lessons from University of Arizona coach Jim Gault. Being around the college girls was great fun. They'd say, "Hey, Kerri, try this," and show me new moves I couldn't wait to try.

Lisa, who is eight years older, showed promise as a gymnast by the time she turned 13.

She decided to train full-time away from home, first in Oregon, then a summer in Houston with Bela Karolyi, and later in Oklahoma City.

My heart broke when she left home. I missed her so much, especially at night because I used to crawl into her bed with her when I was scared or had trouble sleeping. I didn't understand why she wanted to leave me. I cried for days.

The summer I turned seven, my parents took Lisa to Houston to attend Bela's summer camp. I tagged along in what would be my first of many trips there.

While my parents toured the gym for the first time, I started practicing back flips on the mats.

One of Bela's coaches saw me and told my parents they should leave me there, too.

"We can make her an Olympic champion!" he said.

My parents weren't ready to turn both daughters over to the sport just yet.

I begged to stay. But once again, I had to say a sad goodbye to Lisa.

Another teary time in my early years came in the fourth grade. I worked six months on a school science project, determined to win first prize.

My brother drove me to school with my project, a large aquarium-biosphere, in the back of our station wagon.

On the way, Kevin slammed on the brakes to avoid a car. The aquarium slid into the back seat and shattered, tossing frogs, fish, water, and dirt everywhere.

Six months of work was destroyed in seconds.

I called Mom in tears, and

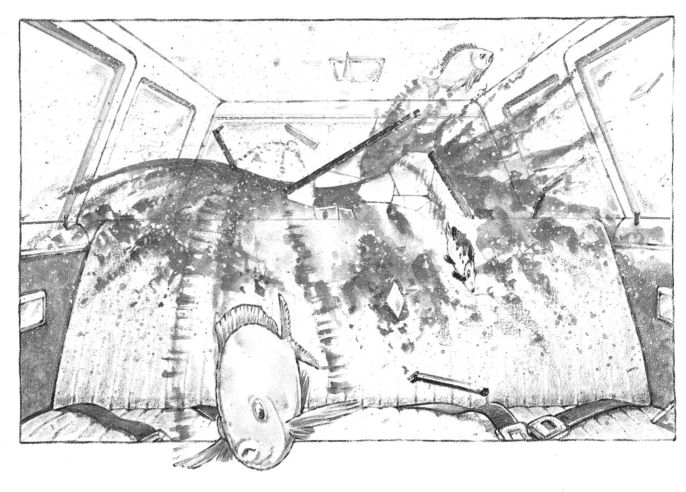

she bailed me out by bringing another aquarium to school.

I remember telling Mom: "This is the worst day of my life."

I'll never forget her response. She said, "I'll be happy if this is your worst day."

Mom always had a way of keeping life's events in perspective. That's one lesson that took me a long time to learn. And things turned out OK; I ended up with second place.

In school, I was always the smallest in my class. I longed to be taller. Even when I reached high school, a few kids would tease me about my 4-foot, 9½-inch height and high-pitched voice.

"What are you doing in high school? Aren't you in elementary school?" they'd joke.

The teasing didn't bother me much because I discovered I could stand tall in the gym. Even today people comment on my voice. I've learned to accept the way I am and laugh along.

I started competing at age eight in the Class III division. In the beginning, I won almost every event I entered. I jumped to the advanced optionals and state competitions. Within a few years I moved up to the Junior Elite level. I competed in my first international competition at 12 and finished third. I also won the Junior B National Championship in 1989.

Nobody competes at the top level overnight, and I was no different. For every step forward, I took a few backward steps before realizing my potential.

Kerri and Dominique Dawes (center) place first and second in a 1990 Junior meet.

Soon people were telling me I could be an Olympian if I trained full time.

Actually, the Olympic seed had been planted years before when I was six. I remember watching Mary Lou Retton win a gold medal at the 1984 Los Angeles Games. I'd watch her winning vault on video over and over—and dream that one day I could do the same.

Mary Lou Retton earned the USA's first ever individual all-around gold medal at the 1984 Olympics. She secured the victory with a perfect 10 in the final event—the vault. The 16-year-old's courageous finish and bubbly smile captured the hearts of fans around the world.

AP/Wide World photos

I never went into gymnastics thinking of it as a career. I did it because I loved it.

But slowly, as I improved, my family and I knew I would have to move away to reach my goals.

At first, my parents discouraged me from moving away from home. Soon, however, they realized that I needed the chance to pursue my dreams, which could not be fulfilled if I stayed at home.

Thanks to Lisa's experiences in gymnastics, we knew what to expect. My parents begrudgingly let me leave home at age 13 to train at Bela's in Houston. Before I left I had to promise to follow two main rules.

The first rule: I had to attend school while training. Many top-level young gymnasts never get far from a gym because tutors come directly to them.

Kerri with one of her best friends, Sunshine Smyth. They have been friends since childhood.

My parents felt it was important for me to be in a school environment. My dad said I wouldn't always have gymnastics, but I'd always have my mind. Being in school helped me realize that sports aren't everything. I made and kept friends outside gymnastics.

Training seven to eight hours a day meant my school day was only four hours of core courses. I'd work out from 7:30 to 10:30 in the morning, go to school from 11:00 to 3:30, and return to the gym that evening from 5:00 to 8:30. I'd study after dinner into the night and then do it all over again.

Although it was difficult, I learned how to manage my time and finished high school a year early with straight A's.

1995 Green Fields Country Day High School Graduation

The second rule: no hasty decision-making based on emotions.

As you can imagine, packing my bags to leave home was tough. I had to say goodbye to my parents, my dogs, Skittles and Sandy, my friends, my doll collection, and a part of my childhood.

From age 13 to 18, I trained at five different places. Making so many changes was hard, but most of the reasons were beyond my control. I stayed with five different host families during that time. Some worked out better than others.

Kerri's room at home in Tucson

There were hundreds of times I wanted to give up. I'd make late-night calls home, crying. I'd feel homesick or depressed about an injury or performance, or I'd be hurt by criticism from a coach.

"OK, this is it. I'm coming home," I'd say convincingly.

I had a tendency to blow things out of proportion then, as if the world would end the next day.

That's when my parents would call upon their 24-hour rule.

That meant I had to wait 24 hours before making important decisions. It's a great rule. By the next day, I would have calmed down and found the courage to continue. If I still felt strongly about something the next day, then we could talk about a change.

Staying at Bela's worked out the best for me. One reason was my Aunt Ann and Uncle Don lived in Houston, and I'd visit them on Sundays. They became my second parents.

Every couple of weeks Mom would fly out to see me. I'd see the rest of my family at competitions or over the holidays.

Because my dad is a heart surgeon, we lived a comfortable life and we were fortunate to go on several family vacations. Thoughts and pictures of those happy times kept me going through the years I lived away from home.

It was nice to have the constant reminder that no matter what happened in gymnastics, I always had a family who loved me. I'd take that over medals any day.

Soon the hard work at Bela's began to pay off. At 13, I became the youngest female to win an event title when I took first in the vault at the USA Gymnastics Championships in 1991.

That victory made me believe I could compete with the best in the world, and I started setting goals for the 1992 Olympics.

I returned to Houston and focused on training. As the meets became more important, however, problems surfaced.

I trained with Kim Zmeskal, and she deservedly received most of the attention. In the big meets, she'd stick everything. I always seemed to fall short of my goals.

I started putting extra pressure on myself and was feeling more nervous before meets. In the practice gym, my routines were just as strong as everyone else's. During meets, I'd worry about how others performed and compare myself to them. And if I made a major mistake, it would wreck my entire meet.

As the Olympics drew near, I found myself feeling pangs of jealousy toward Kim and her successes.

Kerri training at Bela Karolyi's in Houston

Gymnasts at the 1992 U.S. Olympic Trials march onto the floor. Participants included: Kerri, Kim Zmeskal, Wendy Bruce, Hilary Grivich, Dominique Dawes, Kim Kelly, Shannon Miller, Amanda Borden, Kristen McDermott, Elisabeth Crandall, Traci Sommer, Juliet Bangerter, Sarah Balogach, Michelle Campi.

Kerri with Trent Dimas, Gold Medal Olympian on high bar.

The U.S. Trials were taxing on my nerves, but I managed to make the 1992 Olympic team as the youngest member at age 14.

The 1992 games in Barcelona were a wonderful experience. Meeting the world's greatest athletes, including the original basketball Dream Team, was a thrill in itself. Luckily, I'm a better gymnast than photographer. My parents bought me a fancy camera to take to Spain. I shot rolls and rolls of film. Unfortunately, I discovered later I incorrectly loaded the film in my camera. I was so upset. I did manage to get a shot of me with American gymnast Trent Dimas.

Besides helping the team earn a bronze medal, my goal was to make the All-Around Finals. Only the top three gymnasts from each team advance. I missed the finals by .014 of a point with Kim taking the team's last spot.

Failing to make the all-around was a huge letdown. It's the main reason I stayed in the sport through the 1996 Games in Atlanta.

However disappointed I felt, our team's heart went out to Kim. As the world champion, she was expected to win gold in Barcelona. But a fall on the balance beam during team competition affected her concentration and a step out-of-bounds during the floor exercise in the All-Around competition spoiled her meet.

I learned a lot from Kim, seeing how she reacted and recovered from her fall. She displayed true sportsmanship. She showed awesome courage by handling the pressures gracefully.

Kim Zmeskal

Left to right: Betty Okino, Wendy Bruce, Dominique Dawes, Shannon Miller, Kerri Strug, Kim Zmeskal

Kim and Kerri at the 1995 World Gymnastics Team Final Banquet in Austin, Texas

A knee injury prevented her from making a comeback, but she didn't hide from the sport.

The year and a half leading up to Atlanta, she was a great friend and provided endless encouragement. When I returned to Bela's, she'd visit the gym and keep me going. Kim would write me notes, or we'd go out for frozen yogurt and just talk. Kim's a skilled listener, and I had plenty of frustrations to get out.

Two injuries after Barcelona almost sapped my energy for gymnastics.

A nagging stomach pain became a concern in early 1993. At first, my coaches wanted me to work through it and questioned my tolerance level.

During that time I met my idol, Mary Lou Retton, at an exhibition meet and told her about my problem. She said I needed to take care of myself and not let coaches talk me into competing if I wasn't ready.

I should have followed her advice. Shortly thereafter, I ripped my stomach muscles at a meet in Europe. It hurt to breathe.

My parents brought me home to monitor the situation. The injury kept me out of training for six months. I stayed at home for another year and trained in Tucson while I finished high school classes. Top national coaches would visit me every few weeks as I trained on my own.

The time off from regular workouts provided a good change. It helped me regroup and made me eager to compete again.

Just as I started progressing, however, another injury threatened my career in the summer of 1994.

On a hot August night in Palm Springs, California, I suffered a terrifying fall from the uneven bars. While attempting a simple required move, I failed to re-grab the high bar.

The padded mats did little to soften my free fall. My chest and chin hit the mat first while my legs rotated behind in an unnatural backbend.

I lay motionless a few minutes, almost in a daze from the shock and pain. I finally moved my arms to show the paramedics where I hurt most. I wore a neck brace as they carried me off on a stretcher to a hospital.

I stayed in the hospital a couple of days while doctors tested my back.

Fortunately, I didn't need surgery, but the fall did leave me with a badly sprained back.

I started physical therapy within days because the World Team Championships were just two months away.

I lifted weights and did special stretching exercises. Rebuilding my back strength took many hours of painful effort. Bouncing back mentally took even longer and hurt worse.

In competition, every top-level gymnast must perform the same move I fell on. I knew I'd have to master it again to continue in gymnastics. But what if I missed again?

Attempting the move after my injury took all of the courage I could produce.

I got over it by forcing myself to remember the times I did it successfully rather than dwell on the one time I messed up. Having coaches standing by, ready to catch me, helped too. Soon, with repeated successes, my fears faded.

In a strange way, the fall helped me rise to a new level. Surviving that setback taught me how to manage my fears.

I believe we all have fears. I found that by thinking positively and talking to myself, I'm able to push away my feelings of despair.

Performing on the balance beam gives you no option but to force out fear. Tumbling on a four-inch wide beam is never easy. If I thought about falling, I probably would.

Instead, I focus on doing the best routine possible, and I calm myself with reassuring self-talk. "You can do this. You've done it a million times."

Two months after my fall, I made it to the 1994 Team World Championships and helped Team USA finish second in the meet.

About the same time, I figured out that I had to stop comparing myself to others.

I slowly realized I couldn't control what others did or said, so why worry about it?

The only person I can control is me.

I'm a perfectionist by nature, which is both a strength and a weakness. It made me work hard to succeed, but I became my own worst enemy when I failed.

I guess I learned how to balance that driving force inside and how to give myself a break when everything didn't go as planned.

During my career, I've competed all across America and in seven different countries.

I've had travel delays, cancellations and last-minute changes of plan, all of which can be upsetting.

Even the sport of gymnastics can be a soap opera at times, with various people involved with all sorts of things.

As an athlete, those situations were beyond my control. My best advice is to "go with the flow" when you face uncertainty.

There will be times when you are tempted to go against the flow—times you want to break out of your routine.

I know all about that. Our daily training wasn't exciting at all: gymnastics, school, gymnastics, study, sleep—over and over.

When we went to competitions, sometimes we'd imagine great escapes from the hotels and away from the watchful eyes of our coaches. We knew we'd never do it because we didn't want to suffer the consequences of breaking the rules. But it was fun thinking about how we'd explore new cities on our own.

I mention this to show you how all of us toy with the idea of doing crazy things. It's important to separate reality and fantasy. It takes a special courage and determination to walk the narrow path to success day by day and stay out of trouble.

L.M. Otero/ AP photo

I could begin to see my goal of returning to the Olympics in sight by 1995.

I won the All-Around at the U.S. Olympic Festival in Colorado Springs that year and scored well in the other big meets.

Judges are human, and, like most people, you have to earn their respect. In gymnastics competitions, that comes through consistent performances. It can take years before they reward you with high scores. As one of the senior members on the U.S. team, I started to feel judges were giving me respect and the scores I needed.

AP/Wide World Photos

Did you know gymnastics officials change scoring rules every four years? That usually means gymnasts must complete increasingly more difficult routines to score high marks.

Nadia Comaneci scored the first perfect 10 in Olympic history at the 1976 Games in Montreal on the uneven bars. She won three gold medals with six more 10s. If she executed the same routines perfectly in Atlanta, her scores would have been significantly lower.

Kerri, Martha and Bela Karolyi

Bela Karolyi coached Nadia Comaneci before leaving communist Romania for freedom in America. He also coached Mary Lou Retton.

By the end of 1995, I decided to return to Bela and his wife, Martha, in Houston. Their ways were more disciplined and harder than my previous coach's, but I wasn't afraid of the hard work and long hours.

I figured training with Bela would give me the best chance to win a medal in Atlanta and to compete in the all-around.

After switching to Bela, I won the America's Cup All-Around title, my first International All-Around crown since joining the senior elite level. That victory gave me a huge confidence boost.

William R. Sallaz/Duomo

Despite my second-place finish in the all-around and first-place finishes in the floor and vault at the U.S. Trials, Shannon Miller, Dominique Dawes, and Dominique Moceanu received most of the pre-Olympic spotlight. That didn't bother me. I was focused on the games.

I knew hype didn't matter. Only performance.

My plan was to do the best I could for the team, make all-around finals, hopefully bring home some medals, then compete in collegiate gymnastics at UCLA, like my sister. I saw how much fun my sister had being on her college team and looked forward to that experience.

In Atlanta, I felt the magic of team chemistry.

Our Atlanta coaches—Martha Karolyi and Mary Lee Tracy—did a terrific job of unifying our Olympic team. They set the "team" tone leading up to the games.

By the start of competition, everyone pulled for each other. Everyone set aside personal goals and past jealousies to strive for the gold medal.

After the first night of competition, in which we all did the same routines, we trailed the first-place Russian team 193.796 to 193.669.

Two nights later everyone was free to do her own routine. We started hot on the uneven bars with everyone performing well. By the time we moved to the beam, we led the Russians by four-tenths of a point. We doubled that margin after the floor exercise for a comfortable lead going into our final event—the vault.

Our first four vaulters posted solid scores. Moceanu needed a 9.7 to clinch the gold, but two falls on her landing hushed the "USA, USA" chants from the crowd of 32,000 in the Georgia Dome. She received a 9.2.

Even though I was the last to vault, I wasn't aware of the exact score. Still, I could feel the gold slipping away.

The vault is my strength. I hadn't missed my difficult twisting vault, with a 1½ twist, the past three months, so I had confidence.

But just like Moceanu, I landed short on my first vault and fell backward. The moment my feet hit the floor I heard a pop. As I scrambled to stand, a fiery pain shot up my left leg.

When I tried to walk, my ankle felt loose, as if it would fall off. I tried to shake it out as I limped down the runway.

I heard Bela yelling, "You can do it!"

I stared back with eyes ready to burst, thinking to myself, "I don't know if I can do this. Something is wrong."

By the time I reached the end of the runway and turned, my thoughts turned positive. As the adrenaline raced through my blood, I thought to myself:

"You can do this! You've done it a million times. You're ready."

Everyone was counting on me. I owed it to them to try.

Then, I said a little prayer: "Please, God, help me out here."

Amazingly, the pain eased. I sprinted pain-free to the springboard. After a quick twisting blur, I landed on both feet and heard another snap. I lifted the throbbing ankle, balanced on one foot to salute the judges, then collapsed to my knees. The vault earned a 9.712 score.

Barton Silverman/NYT Pictures

John Gaps III/AP Photo

The crowd erupted! Camera flashbulbs exploded. The gold medal was ours! Martha and Barb (our Olympic trainer) carried me off to doctors, who placed me on a stretcher, examined my ankle, and then wrapped it.

At first, officials advised I be taken immediately to the hospital. I pleaded with the doctors and the coaches to let me stay for the awards ceremony. Bela agreed and hoisted me off the stretcher and carried me in his arms to the stand for the medal presentation.

I felt a mixture of emotions. I worried about my ankle, but mostly I felt overwhelming pride for our team and country.

I found out later that our team would have clinched the gold without my second vault. It didn't matter to me.

I needed the second vault to qualify for the all-around, and I didn't want to end my Olympics with a fall.

The important thing is I believed in myself and went after my dreams when it mattered the most. I believe all of my teammates would've done the same thing.

The following days I spent every waking hour in physical therapy trying to nurse my ankle back to health. I prayed for a miraculous recovery in time for the individual events.

The injury spoiled my dream of competing in the all-around.

When Bela told me "No go" just before the individual apparatus competition, I was crushed.

I remember going back to my room in Atlanta where Mom comforted me.

"But I didn't get all of my goals," I said with tears flowing.

"Well, Kerri, sometimes we don't always reach all our goals," Mom said. "That's part of life."

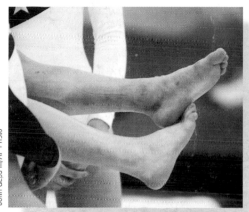

I did manage to tumble gingerly with teammates in a farewell exhibition to close the gymnastics competition. That's when I first realized my final vault touched people in a special way. Maybe I had reached beyond my goals after all.

New opportunities arose and I suddenly needed a new courage to face difficult career decisions, like giving up my amateur status and college gymnastics to turn professional.

All types of attention have been poured my way. I've made the talk-show rounds and met many famous people. I know fame can be fleeting, so I'm enrolled at UCLA and plan to assist their gymnastics program to give something back to the sport that has taught me so much.

I look back on all that's happened, and I know my final vault inspired many people. Maybe I reminded people that the courage to soar to great heights is inside all of us. If you work hard, be persistent, and follow your dreams—anyone can have a heart of gold.